Career Quest

EXPLORING ENVIRONMENTAL SCIENCES CAREERS

SHERRY HOWARD

TWENTY-FIRST CENTURY BOOKS / MINNEAPOLIS

Twenty-First Century Books™
An imprint of Lerner Publishing Group, Inc.
241 First Avenue North
Minneapolis, MN 55401 USA

For reading levels and more information, look up this title at www.lernerbooks.com.

Main body text set in Bembo Std Regular.
Typeface provided by Monotype Typography.

Library of Congress Cataloging-in-Publication Data

Names: Howard, Sherry, author.
Title: Exploring environmental sciences careers / Sherry Howard.
Description: Minneapolis : Twenty-First Century Books, [2026] | Series: Career quest | Includes bibliographical references and index. | Audience: Ages 11–18 | Audience: Grades 7–9 | Summary: "The environmental sciences are a broad field perfect for anyone interested in Earth's environment and ecosystems. From studying weather to becoming a parker ranger, learn more about these careers and how to secure one"— Provided by publisher.
Identifiers: LCCN 2024037262 (print) | LCCN 2024037263 (ebook) | ISBN 9798765644188 (lib. bdg.) | ISBN 9798765684887 (paperback) | ISBN 9798765682777 (epub)
Subjects: LCSH: Environmental sciences—Vocational guidance—Juvenile literature.
Classification: LCC GE60 .H69 2026 (print) | LCC GE60 (ebook) | DDC 550.23—dc23/eng/20250110

LC record available at https://lccn.loc.gov/2024037262
LC ebook record available at https://lccn.loc.gov/2024037263

Manufactured in the United States of America
1 – CG – 7/15/25

CONTENTS

INTRODUCTION 4

CHAPTER ONE
ALL ABOUT THE ENVIRONMENTAL SCIENCES 6

CHAPTER TWO
CAREER PATHS IN THE ENVIRONMENTAL SCIENCES 14

CHAPTER THREE
CAREER EXPLORATION 28

CHAPTER FOUR
GETTING STARTED WITH YOUR CAREER 36

CHAPTER FIVE
THE FUTURE 47

CONCLUSION
A SPOT FOR EVERYONE 54

Glossary 56
Source Notes 58
Selected Bibliography 59
Further Information 60
Index 62

INTRODUCTION

Have you ever wondered what job interests you enough that you'd like to work it every day—possibly for the rest of your working life? While it may seem too early to begin thinking about career paths, middle and high school are ideal times to start thinking about jobs and building skills in your area of interest.

So what *does* interest you? This book is a guide on careers in the environmental sciences. This broad field covers studying the environment, how humans impact it, and environmental concerns. It includes all kinds of disciplines, from ecology (the study of relationships between organisms and their environment) to meteorology (the study of atmosphere and weather) to environmental engineering. There are many jobs in this field, and one of them may be a perfect fit for you. This book will help you explore and make decisions while still in school to figure out if a career in environmental science is right for you and, if so, to achieve your career goals as quickly as possible. You'll learn what the careers are in the field, what it takes to secure a job, what the average pay range is, whether you need to attend college, and more.

Environmental scientists protect the environment and human health.

CHAPTER ONE

All about the Environmental Sciences

The environment is the surroundings or conditions in which we live, such as nature, the climate, Earth's ecosystems, or even our homes. When talking about the environmental sciences, the focus is on Earth and the natural world. There are many ways to study environmental sciences. Some people specialize in the natural environment, such as forestry or animal biology, while others focus on human-influenced fields, such as agriculture or public health.

Have you ever considered what it is about the environment that is important to you? Maybe you are worried about the state of Earth's clean air. Perhaps you love penguins and want to help preserve their natural habitat. Or you might wonder about the forests and other ecosystems that we've lost as urban centers grow. If you think about the environment often or want to work to help keep it healthy, then you may be heading for a career in the environmental sciences. You may even be surprised by the careers you'll find in this discipline. It is a broad field that involves most skill sets and interests.

Hundreds of king penguins surround a wildlife biologist in the Crozet Islands. Wildlife biology is part of the environmental sciences.

History of Environmental Science Careers

Since the development of agriculture around twelve thousand years ago, there have been people whose job was to care for crops and animals. Those people created the earliest known environmental science careers. They might not have called it science back then. But understanding what the soil needed to grow successful harvests, which foods to feed their livestock, and how to ensure the land would be healthy for future crops was all part of environmental science.

Many environmental science careers are specifically related to environmentalism, which focuses on preserving, restoring, and improving the natural environment. Environmentalism has been around for generations too. Indigenous people have always been stewards of the land on which they live and the animals that call that place home, helping to preserve and protect the balance of those ecosystems. Ancient Romans sometimes reused broken pottery rather than throwing it away. People in ancient China encouraged limiting water use, protecting young tree growth, and practicing sustainable fishing. As early as 1720, hundreds of Bishnoi people in India were killed while trying to protect trees from the Maharaja (ruler) of Jodhpur, India, who wanted to cut them down to build a palace. The Bishnoi, who practice a type of Hinduism, are forbidden from harming trees and animals due to their faith. Many people call them the first environmentalists of India. "We save nature, and nature saves us," one contemporary member said in a 2018 interview.

The concept of environmental science careers, especially those related to environmentalism, as we know them became more mainstream during the 1960s. People began discussing the use of Earth's limited resources such as oil and timber more. The media reported more about the environmental crisis, discussing car emissions, oil spills, and pollution. In 1962 Rachel Carson published *Silent Spring*. The environmental science book documented the harm the pesticide DDT does to the environment, as well as the false information the chemical industry spread to the American public about DDT being safe. In response, more people wanted to preserve our natural world.

Residents of Sydney, Australia, protest motor vehicle pollution at a 1972 Friends of Earth march.

They tried to save threatened and endangered species. Efforts to control pollution and waste grew.

In response to the increasing interest in environmentalism, the United States, and much of the world, celebrated its first Earth Day in 1970. Later that year, the Environmental Protection Agency (EPA) was founded. For the first time, people were needed to conduct research, write laws and standards to protect people and the land, fight pollution, and advise the US president on environmentalism and the environmental sciences.

A graduate student examines seeds in a campus greenhouse. In 1969 the University of Virginia founded the first Department of Environmental Sciences that offered bachelor's through doctoral degrees.

Environmental Science Careers Take Off

New environmental legislation helped career opportunities in the environmental sciences grow. For instance, in 1972 the Clean Water Act was enacted. This act regulated the types of pollutants released into water and set water quality standards. Before there were no governmental standards for water used for swimming, fishing, and drinking. People and companies often dumped waste into waterways without a second thought. With this new act, the demand for workers who specialized in this area expanded. The EPA hired engineers to impose quality controls and protect our waters.

Congress passed the Environmental Response, Compensation, and Liability Act in 1980, a toxic waste cleanup law. As a result, scientists, engineers, and researchers were needed to study toxic waste concerns and find solutions.

In addition to needing workers to help with legislative changes, overall growing awareness about the environment made more people want to work in the environmental sciences. And as more people wanted to work in the environmental sciences, the field branched into the disciplines that many environmental sciences are still in. These include climate; wildlife; sustainability; environmental health, safety, and education; and environmental engineering. However, these disciplines also often overlap and transform as world conditions change. For instance, a natural disaster or other event may cause a redistribution of resources, which includes workers. In response, workers may need to change locations for their careers. Or they may need to switch to working in a different but related field. For example, an environmental scientist could work primarily in a lab researching ways to clean water for human consumption but be called to work in the field instead if a huge toxic waste event, such as a factory's illegal dumping of toxins, struck their location's only drinkable water source.

People Who Choose Careers in Environmental Science

What kind of people tend to be attracted to jobs in the environmental sciences? Many careers in the field require a strong interest in science or math. Maybe you've enjoyed those classes in school. Maybe you love to solve problems. These are key skills in any environmental science.

Have you followed the plight of endangered species and

Important Voice in Environmental Science

George Washington Carver was a Black agricultural scientist who was born enslaved in 1864 in Missouri. He became free after the United States abolished slavery in 1865. Carver pursued an education and spent time traveling and learning about plants and their properties. In 1885 he was accepted at Highland College in Kansas, but when the college learned he was Black, they revoked his application. Eventually, he would attend Simpson College in Iowa, and, after transferring to current-day Iowa State University, he earned bachelor's and master's degrees. He was the first Black man in the United States to have a graduate degree in agricultural science.

Carver worked for the Tuskegee Institute in Alabama, a historically Black university. He wanted to improve the life of Black people through education and skill-building, especially through farming. He later became famous for his work in soil conservation and sustainable farming practices.

Carver saw that soil health could be nurtured and cared for. He knew that we could avoid using up some natural resources by nurturing their health. He taught about crop rotation, which is when someone grows a series of different crops in one area across a series of growing seasons to help improve soil health. His work shaped modern agricultural conservation. Carver is considered one of the best agricultural scientists of all time. His work with soil health and conservation helped many directly, and his research continues to help people all over the world.

Marine biologists are a type of environmental scientist. They study oceans and the plants and animals that live in them.

want to know what you can offer to help protect and preserve those species? Maybe you've adopted an animal through a nonprofit organization such as the World Wildlife Fund, contributing a monthly amount to support research relating to that animal. If your hobby, job, volunteer work, or other activities focus on the environment, maybe that's telling you something about a potential career choice. If you enjoy tracking weather, spending time at state or national parks, or learning about different ecosystems, that could be a sign too. Or if it's important to you to recycle, pick up litter, conserve electricity, or otherwise reduce your environmental impact, you might find a career focusing on that in one of the many areas of environmental science.

Many environmental science careers overlap. And careers can change as Earth and its environment change. Regardless of what branch someone goes into, the environmental sciences offer opportunities for people of all genders, abilities, and education levels.

CHAPTER TWO

Career Paths in the Environmental Sciences

So many opportunities await in the environmental sciences. No matter what area of the environment you care most about, there's likely a career path forward. From weather to wildlife, people who choose careers in the environmental sciences devote themselves to understanding, protecting, or studying the environment.

Careers that benefit the environment or help conserve natural resources are also called green careers. Although not all, many careers in the environmental sciences are green careers. These are jobs that involve the environment, conservation, or preservation. It is estimated that by 2030 green careers will comprise around 14 percent of all jobs in the United States. The fastest-growing green jobs include wind turbine service technicians, solar panel installers, and electricians. Classifying green jobs and environmental sciences can be difficult, as some jobs overlap with other sectors such as general engineering too.

Researching how to grow crops sustainably is a green career.

Environmental Science Careers Related to Climate

Climate scientists study Earth's climate. Many careers fall under that broad heading. Let's take a look at a few of them.

Meteorologist. The person you see on television reporting the weather might be a meteorologist. These skilled weather experts can use tools such as radar, mapping, and satellites to predict the weather. Meteorologists can also teach as atmospheric scientists. They can consult on investigations that involve property damage, give testimony on weather-related events, help airlines map flight paths, and forecast the weather. Many organizations, including government agencies and news stations, employ them. The median salary for a meteorologist in 2023 was $92,860.

Energy auditor. An energy auditor's job is to figure out how energy is used in homes and businesses. They help you learn how to make the best use of resources and conserve energy. Conserving energy can help people reduce their utility bills. Some utility companies offer energy audits to residences and businesses. With the help of an energy auditor, building owners can find ways to be more energy efficient. The average energy auditor earns $73,212.

Weatherization expert. A weatherization expert is likely to follow up after the work of an energy auditor. They work with people and businesses to correct air leaks, control moisture, and protect buildings from wind. They also help people harness the power of the sun by installing solar panels to collect energy. This career is hands-on, with workers receiving practical, on-the-job training.

Disaster preparedness trainer or responder. These workers focus on emergency preparedness and responses to emergencies. Climate emergencies are on the rise. The EPA employs such professionals, as part of the agency's job is knowing how to respond to a natural or human-made disaster and researching response improvements. The United States Geological Survey focuses on emergency readiness as well, communicating any potential risks, impacts, and ways to save lives during floods, tsunamis, hurricanes, and other disasters. The national median salary for emergency preparedness coordinators in 2022 was $79,186.

Climatologist. These professionals study the weather patterns that make up a region's climate. Many of them focus on patterns relative to air pollution. They might work for government agencies or perform climate research. All climatologists must have a bachelor's degree. They also need

Soil science is a growing green career. Studying the relationship between people and the environment can help reduce the effects of climate change.

a master's degree to work in government or a doctorate to complete advanced research. The median salary in 2023 was $92,860.

Global issues such as climate change are making the climate sector of the environmental sciences grow rapidly. These careers are only a sampling of available opportunities. People are needed to study our climate and the human impact on it and to help find ways to reduce or change that impact.

Environmental Science Careers Related to Wildlife

Careers that focus on wildlife might appeal to people who love animals, parks, or the outdoors. If that sounds like you, you may want to take a deeper look at some of these career paths. The people who choose these careers want to maintain healthy and safe habitats for animals. This requires the combined efforts of scientists, educators, enforcement officers, forensic specialists, and many other workers. Let's take a look at a few of the careers that focus on wildlife.

Animal welfare. This career field focuses on keeping animals safe, including taking care of them and ensuring their future protection. People who work to prevent the extinction of endangered species are also in this field. Some examples of animal welfare professionals include zoologists and animal

Around twenty thousand people work in the National Park Service.

History of the National Park Service

America's national parks are living laboratories. Take a peek at the history of the park system:

1831 Painter George Catlin painted Indigenous people in their ancestral land. He created 470 portraits of forty different nations. His environmental art preserved Indigenous ways of life and expanded public knowledge of Indigenous nations and land.

1872 Thanks to environmental scientists and writers such as John Muir, Clarence King, and John Wesley Powell, Americans learned about the scenic landscapes of the western United States. Additionally, Congress created Yellowstone National Park. This park stretches through 2,000,000 acres (809,371 ha) of Montana and Wyoming.

1876 The first private conservation organization, the Appalachian Mountain Club, formed. Members vowed to explore and preserve the White Mountains of New Hampshire. They encourage everyday people to be community scientists in national parks and beyond.

1958 The oldest predator-prey study began in Isle Royale National Park, tracking moose and wolf populations. Ecologist and conservationist Durward Allen started the project in 1958. He hoped the study would protect future wolf populations. Allen died in 1997, but the study continues.

1972 The first urban national parks were introduced. Later, Urban Park Rangers were appointed. They are environmental scientists who help city dwellers learn about the natural world.

1999–2001 Research Learning Centers were created to encourage research in national parks and share their results with both park managers and the public.

Working for Change

The United Nations Environment Programme (UNEP) is a leading global authority on the environment. For more than fifty years, this organization has worked on many areas of environmentalism, from promoting green economies to finding the root of problems such as pollution and biodiversity loss to protecting the land and water. Every June 5, a country involved in UNEP hosts World Environment Day, which encourages people to take action in protecting the environment. UNEP works with organizations in many different sectors and scientific disciplines to figure out the most effective ways to make change. Environmental scientists who specialize in areas such as resource management, climate change, and environmental engineering are key to the program's success.

researchers. These two animal welfare careers had a median salary of $70,600 in 2023.

Wildlife manager or game warden. These professionals enforce programs that protect wildlife and their habitats. Game wardens often have law enforcement authority similar to—or even greater than—that of police officers, conducting searches of vehicles or people of interest in an effort to protect humans, animals, and natural resources. Their median salary was $60,380 in 2023.

Habitat conservationist. Careers in this field encompass forests, parks, rangelands, and more. Habitat conservationists help manage the land quality and conserve life in these habitats. They may work for governments, individuals, or places such as nature reserves or wildlife parks. The 2023 median salary was $68,300.

Park ranger. The United States Department of the Interior offers a career path as a park ranger. These rangers are considered the ambassadors for public parks. If you'd like to protect the natural and cultural history that state and national parks preserve, this career might interest you. A park ranger might make between $39,576 and $51,446 per year.

Endangered species protection or wildlife inspector and forensics specialist. These careers offer an opportunity to combine the work of a sleuth and a conservationist. Some of these jobs allow you to investigate the smuggling of wild animals and their body parts. Forensics specialists in the field work at locations such as ports and border crossings to intercept illegal wildlife goods. The median salary for forensic science technicians was $64,940 in 2023. Criminal investigators who work for the US Customs and Border Protection have the potential for higher earnings.

Environmental Science Careers Related to Sustainability

Sustainability, which refers to methods of harvesting or using resources that avoid permanently damaging or depleting them, is a common buzzword. You might see it on packaging or in advertisements. To try to achieve sustainability, some grocery stores provide recycling bins for used shopping bags. People may

In 2024 there were 3.1 million workers in the clean energy sector working in all fifty states.

carry their own metal or biodegradable straws or otherwise skip using a plastic one to avoid single-use plastic. School lunches may be served on biodegradable trays.

There are also many careers in sustainability. Careers that focus on sustainability have huge appeal for people who specifically want to focus on the depletion of natural resources. Because of that depletion, habitat loss, air pollution, and other risks increase yearly, which means there are more individuals and organizations working to reverse the damage. Let's look at two careers that focus on sustainability:

Community planner. Cities are always growing. But there is more to urban sprawl than just building more towns or shopping centers. Community planners ensure that residents all over the city have access to public spaces and green spaces. They work with landscape architects to study natural geography and understand the best way to protect and develop the land. Other environmental scientists who specialize in water pollution, air quality, and soil contamination may be pulled into community planning as well. Many community planning jobs require a master's degree in urban planning and an undergraduate degree in architecture, engineering, environmental science, or environmental studies. The average salary for an urban and regional planner is $81,800.

Energy management. Energy managers look for the most efficient way to use energy. They may perform audits to monitor energy consumption or consult on new building projects to figure out the best sources of heating, lighting, ventilation, or other systems. They may be hired to check over older buildings and suggest ideas on how to make them more energy efficient. Careers in energy management might focus on wind turbines, solar panels, and biomass developments. The average salary for an energy manager is $97,940.

Environmental Science Careers Related to Environmental Health, Safety, and Education

Careers that focus on environmental health, safety, and education keep people safe from natural and human-made dangers. Governments, nonprofits, and corporations all hire experts in this sector. Most careers require at least a bachelor's degree. But sometimes an associate degree can get you in the door. Salaries in this sector can range from around $60,000 to more than $100,000. Here are a few jobs with this focus:

Air quality engineer. These jobs are about the safety of the air we breathe. Air pollution is a major threat to human and animal health. Every time we breathe, we can inhale pollutants. Air quality engineers measure the amount of pollutants in the air. They come up with solutions to minimize them. They might also work with companies to design ways to reduce contaminants in the air. These jobs are in high demand, and the median salary is around $100,000.

Environmental health and safety specialist. These individuals are experts in the field of health and safety regulations. They monitor environmental protections in the workplace. They collect and analyze data taken from air, soil, water, plant, and other samples. They help improve the health and safety of both indoor and outdoor settings. The median salary in 2023 was $77,580.

Environmental regulations enforcement. These careers will usually be in government. Most countries have an agency that oversees laws that protect the environment. In the United States, the EPA employs professionals to keep the air, land, and inhabitants free from hazardous waste and to monitor and enforce compliance with environmental laws. Compliance officers need at least a four-year degree to get started, and a more advanced degree is required to enter more specialized fields, such as one in ecology, environmental science, chemistry, or environmental engineering. Additional certifications may be needed depending on the field in which they work. Because there is such a wide range of roles, locations, and required education, salaries range from $66,000 to $97,000.

Public health educator. The environment plays a huge role in a community's health. Have you ever heard the

Public health educators work with communities to promote awareness about important issues.

warnings to stay indoors on a day with bad air quality? People depend on those warnings to help make sure they aren't inhaling too many pollutants, especially if they have a health condition such as asthma. The warnings come from someone who has chosen a career in public health education. Public health educators also manage illnesses and their spread. For example, during the beginning of the COVID-19 pandemic, many public health educators were needed to monitor COVID protocols and their effectiveness. The median salary for 2023 was $62,860, although some positions require advanced degrees and therefore usually pay more. People with doctorates in public health train students, conduct research, and consult for programs interested in high-quality public health.

Environmental Science Careers Related to Engineering

Engineers work in almost all career paths relating to the environment. The following two engineering jobs might be of special interest to you if you're interested in disaster relief, agriculture, or soil health.

Environmental engineer. Some engineering graduates choose to start a career with agencies that bring disaster relief. They figure out best practices for wastewater management, air purification, waste disposal, and structure analysis. After natural disasters, they look at what caused them and how they can be prevented in the future. They also study infrastructure—how could it be strengthened or improved? Were there factors, such as bridge failure or road damage, that added to the destruction? The average salary is $100,190.

Green Money

Green careers can pay very well. According to 2023 data from the US Bureau of Labor Statistics, the top earners in green careers were scientists and engineers. Geoscientists (people who study the physical makeup of Earth), microbiologists (people who study microscopic organisms, the way they live and grow, and how they interact with their environments), epidemiologists (people who study causes of disease and injury and any related patterns), and general environmental scientists earned the most. In 2023 the median wage was at least $75,000 for each of these, depending on position and education.

Civil engineer. Civil engineers are involved with planning public works and utilities, such as roadways, bridges, water supplies, pollution control, and more. They make sure new builds work with natural ecosystems and existing infrastructure. Joan Dietsch, a civil engineering major at the University of Notre Dame, chose her major because it combined her two interests: soil science and math. She explains, "All infrastructure, everything civil engineers work on, rests upon soil and is influenced by the soil structure and properties at a particular site. In this way, I could keep my interests in soil alive, but also study the math and engineering processes that I had come to love." In 2023 civil engineers made a median salary of $95,890.

Even More Environmental Science Careers

We've covered a broad sampling of the different kinds of careers available in the environmental sciences. But there are too many to detail every discipline and every job within them. Some additional popular environmental science disciplines that you might want to research include geology (the study of the history of Earth and its life, especially through rocks), ecology, biology (the study of living organisms), marine biology, and more. Many people in these branches work in the field or in labs to research and study their discipline. No matter what part of the environment you think of, there's probably someone in the environmental sciences working to study, understand, help, or improve it.

CHAPTER THREE

Career Exploration

Now that you know about some careers in the environmental sciences, you can think about whether those careers might interest you. You may have already noticed some branches of the field that sound interesting. Matching your interests and preferences to your career should help you find job satisfaction in the future.

During his high school years, Spencer Thompson, the founder of the career-planning platform Sokanu, "noticed a pattern among his classmates when it came to post-graduation plans: they made choices based upon what family or friends thought they should do, rather than their intrinsic passions, capabilities, or potential." Thompson urges students to look inward and to consider options that suit them. You will eventually have to narrow your career options down to a few, but now is the time to explore all the possibilities available. Let's cover some different ways to explore career paths while you're still in school.

It's important to start thinking about and exploring careers while you're still in school.

See What You Can See

Consider the resources available to you as you begin exploring careers in environmental science. Find a trusted adult who can help you. You might ask a guardian, a coach, a school counselor, or a favorite teacher. Or you can explore on your own or with a friend.

Begin by exploring the businesses and organizations in your immediate area. You can use your school's resources and books—such as this one—to consider your career options. You can also check out your public library for career resources. They may have a collection of career- and business-related books and magazines. The Conservation Job Board is the largest career website for environmental science jobs, and the Department of Energy has career maps that guide users through job descriptions, titles, education requirements, salary averages, and more.

Consider keeping a career journal as you begin looking. Your notes will become a valuable resource as you continue on your career journey because you'll be able to reference

Writing down thoughts and ideas can help you achieve goals faster and find areas to improve.

your thoughts, feelings, and research. Some things you may want to journal about are:

- books you read
- sites you visit
- environmental scientists and related professionals you interact with
- events or activities you want to schedule in the future
- careers you want to know more about
- thoughts and feelings about the careers you look into
- art and scribbles that inspire you

Site Visits

Visiting a worksite can help you learn everything you can about the place, including the types of people who work there, the educational requirements for different levels of employment, and whatever other facts you're curious about. These visits can be in person or virtual. For example, you may be interested in becoming a park ranger. To learn more about the job and work environment, you could visit a national or state park. But if you do not have the opportunity to go to one in person, you can visit online instead by taking a virtual tour or watching videos. Or if you're interested in engineering, you could research and find a building, structure, or other project you love and learn about the companies and people who were involved with its construction.

Interview

It is also possible to visit someone and talk to them to learn about their work. One method is by scheduling an informational interview. These meetings let you ask someone about their career to learn more about their daily work, education, skills, and career experience. Choose an area that interests you and think about possible professionals in your area. Maybe you're passionate about air quality—you could reach out to your city's utility office and ask to be connected to a liaison officer. If you love farming, try visiting a local farmer's market and introduce yourself to someone running a stand. How about a visit to a veterinarian, a zoo, or an

The more people you talk to about your career interests, the greater possibility of exploring your passions.

Tell Me All about It

Once you have secured an interview, you could have a friend or family member help you prepare by interviewing them or asking for help writing questions. Here are some sample questions to get you started:

- When did you decide that you wanted this career?
- How long have you been working in this field?
- What kind of education was required?
- How many years were you in school?
- What were your classes like?
- What does a day look like in your job?
- What is your greatest challenge at work?
- What do you love most about your career?
- What advice do you have for me?

aquarium to meet someone who works with animals? You can also ask a trusted adult if they know of anybody in your field of interest. You can ask any of the professionals you meet if they'd be willing to sit down for an interview with you. The contacts you make now could be helpful in the future as you choose a career because these workers can help you learn more about the work and even let you know about job opportunities in the field.

School Clubs

Clubs in your school can also help you explore career options. Does your school have a club that falls under the environmental science umbrella? Examples include—but aren't limited to—the Future Farmers of America, an environmental club, or a green or eco-organization. Other clubs might not be directly related to environmental science but have the ability to make eco-friendly changes, such as student council.

If your school doesn't have a club devoted to the environment, you can probably start one. There are many club activities that can help you learn more about the environment and environmental sciences. You could start a school or community garden, an after-school ecology club, or a recycling drive. Maybe you'll organize a cleanup day and invite environmental science professionals to speak at your school. Or you could lead a school summit to discuss problems facing our natural world and solutions to them.

If you want to start a club, begin with finding a teacher to sponsor you. They can help you through the process required at your school.

Nonprofits and Volunteering

Volunteering can be a great way to try out different types of work. Often, you can work around your schedule and make a small time commitment. Many local animal shelters accept youth volunteers. Local nonprofits often have opportunities for young people to get involved. Or you could volunteer to help scientists collect data through community research. It may take some research to find what's available in your area. Be creative. If no opportunity exists, try to create one.

National or global nonprofit organizations can be great resources for you to learn more about the environmental sciences and become more involved in your community too, even if it's in simple ways. It's good to choose a nonprofit that has a mission that you find interesting or are passionate about—the work there might help you understand more about your field of interest. One such organization you can volunteer for is the Sierra Club, which has millions of members and has been around since 1892. Their mission is to enjoy and protect the wild places of Earth, to practice and promote the responsible use of ecosystems and resources, and to educate and enlist people to help restore and protect the environment.

The National Oceanic and Atmospheric Administration has volunteer opportunities as well. Their citizen science programs train storm spotters, weather observers, or precipitation reporters to track severe weather. They have apps where people can report animal sightings, especially sightings of tagged animals. Their Cooperative Shark Tagging Program is the longest-running shark-tagging program in the world.

No matter how you choose to start exploring careers, remember that you're at the research stage, where you want to learn a little bit about a lot of options. Knowing what to expect from careers in environmental science will help you make informed decisions about your future. Then you'll be ready to learn a lot about the field that interests you most.

CHAPTER FOUR

Getting Started with Your Career

After you've explored some careers, you can start making decisions about your future. You might have known by third grade that you wanted to study air pollution. You may have imagined practicing animal husbandry in an African game preserve. Or maybe marine biology fascinates you, and you dream of working to save the habitat of the axolotl. Regardless of whether you're still interested in your dream career from elementary school, exploring career options has armed you with more information and the chance to narrow down your choices.

Then, once you've made a tentative decision about a career or have a few fields picked out, you can maximize your high school preparation. You can use those years to refine your interests in and out of school. Schools provide a variety of courses that will help you prepare for a career too. Let's take a look at how to narrow down your career options and make the most of your high school education, and what ways to begin your career might follow.

Mentors, guidance counselors, and community leaders are good resources when it comes to making decisions about your future.

What Works for Your Work?

Let's consider some of the factors that helped you focus on a career path. Think about a day at school. Maybe math and science are your favorite classes. Or maybe your favorite part of school is being around others or working in groups. Perhaps you love the creative side of school, such as art, music, or writing. Understanding your preferences can inform your future path. For example, if you like math and working with your hands, being an environmental engineer could be a good career path for you. Or if you like helping people, maybe you'd do well in disaster relief. Choosing classes you enjoy and that connect to your interests in high school can not only help you narrow down your career options but also help you achieve your goals faster because they prepare you for further education or a future career. Plus, they improve your chances of getting admitted to the college or other program of your choice.

School can teach you more about yourself in other ways too. Do you enjoy learning from a book, or do you prefer conducting an experiment in a lab? Would you rather listen to a lecture or view a slideshow presentation? Do your hands need to be busy with tools to help you understand how to use them, or can you learn a skill through written directions? Do you picture yourself doing computer-based research at a desk in an office? Or do you imagine taking water from a stream to see if it's safe for wildlife to drink it? Attending your classes and paying attention to what interests you about them can help answer these questions and inform what kind of work suits your style. Then you can consider whether your work style fits each career you're interested in.

Additional factors that many people consider when they're planning careers are workplace environment, salary, and benefits. Many people want a job with longevity, meaning it lasts a long time and they feel secure in keeping that job. Some people care most about personal values such as their job satisfaction or their impact on the environment.

But finding the right career isn't as simple as looking at a list and checking each item off. It's about how strongly you feel about each aspect and which factors mean the most. For example, maybe you are interested in animals but also want to work outside. In that case, wildlife conservation or being a game

Identifying strengths and weaknesses can help point your career in the right direction.

warden might be appealing. Or maybe you like facts and figures but don't want to work with people. A job that sends you to different sites, such as installing solar panels, could be the answer to meeting both those factors. For the more indoor-inclined person, research or product development positions could keep your head in the numbers and your workload always changing.

Get Creative with Courses

As you get into your junior and senior years of high school, the idea of choosing a forever career might seem daunting.

You aren't alone. According to a recent survey published by Inside Higher Ed, almost half of recent high school graduates did not feel confident about their path forward to further education or a career. The survey says, "Seventy-two percent reported that they were rarely or only sometimes exposed to a variety of career options that could be pursued." Many also reported that they "had five or fewer conversations with teachers or counselors about the various post–high school opportunities available."

Many jobs in environmental science require a bachelor's degree after high school. Those that don't usually require some other kind of further education. That means a high school degree—or a general educational development (GED) obtained later if you don't graduate from high school—is essential for continuing down this path. It's okay if you haven't decided exactly what you want to do as you finish high school. All the classes you take can still help you prepare for a career. High schools all have general school requirements that you must take to graduate—English, math, science, and, in some cases, a second language. You might not be interested in all those subjects. But each can offer you knowledge that will be invaluable to your future career. For example, learning Latin roots in English literature or Latin language courses will make learning scientific names easier, and literature and language classes can make you a better communicator too. The more math and science you take, the more exposure you have to different equations, concepts, and complex problems that you'll use later on in college and beyond.

Don't be afraid to try electives that take you out of your comfort zone too. Woodworking gives you the chance to try

Just because your strengths do not fit within a traditional job description doesn't mean you can't find work in that field that fits you!

out different tools and learn to build things. Performing arts, such as band or choir, increase your self-confidence since you have to perform in front of other people and exercise your creativity. Computer-related classes, such as programming or graphic design, could come in handy later on if you create blueprints as an engineer or build an app to record scientific data.

When building your class schedule, it can be helpful to speak to a guidance counselor to make sure you are on track to graduate on time and that you meet all the prerequisites required by any colleges or other programs you are considering. Once you start thinking about further education, you can also visit colleges that interest you to get a feel for what each might be like. Many colleges can cater tours to your specific interests. You might even be able to talk to a professor or student in the program you're curious about or sit in on a class. Getting a taste of the next step can be a huge motivator for thinking about and preparing for the future.

After High School

Once you obtain a high school degree or GED, many career paths are available. Each path has pros and cons, and it is important to weigh the potential cost of each program and the value of the training you receive compared to the job you want and the requirements to get it.

Apprenticeship. Apprenticeships are on-the-job training and study programs. They pair you with a mentor who will guide you through every step of the way. You can get a taste of what the job is like before financially investing in further education or expensive tools. Or you may go directly from an apprenticeship into a career.

Apprenticeships are usually paid positions. Depending on your location, finding an apprenticeship in your desired area might be difficult. The National Institute of Environmental Health Services and the EPA offer apprenticeship programs in environmental science. Many engineering, conservation, and technician-related fields offer apprenticeships as well. You can find the requirements for apprenticeships and how to apply for them online.

Internship. Internships give you entry-level experience in a career of your choice. You may be paired with a more experienced worker or placed in a specific department, or you may bounce around different areas of the organization. Interning can connect you to people already in the industry. More than half of all internships lead to full-time jobs. However, many internships are also unpaid. That can mean working extra hours at a regular job to pay the bills, especially if you do not have another financial safety net.

Companies usually post internship positions as job listings

on their website and on online job boards. You may also hear about internships through word of mouth—which is why making contacts in the industry is so important! Internships are especially popular among college and university students. Professors and other faculty members often share opportunities among the department. While you don't have to be in college or university to complete an internship, make sure to read the listing carefully since some of them are only available to those students. They want to attract future hires, and they may require a degree for all employees.

Associate's degree. An associate's program at a community or technical college leads to a degree or certification in a specific field. These undergraduate programs typically take two years. Some colleges only offer a general associate's degree in the environmental sciences, while others may offer specialized degrees in agriculture, animal science, agri-business, conversation, geology, horticulture, and more.

Many people use their associate's degree to begin an entry-level job. Others plan to continue to a bachelor's degree. Credits earned toward an associate's degree can usually be applied toward a bachelor's degree later on, and some associate's degrees, especially in environmental science, are even designed to set students up for a future four-year education. The expansion of online degree offerings and asynchronous classes have allowed many students to work at home and at their own pace. If there isn't a community or technical college in your area—or if they don't have a program you're interested in—an online program may be a good fit for you.

Bachelor's degree. Many of the people who want to work in the environmental sciences will earn a bachelor's

A bachelor's degree can open up many possibilities in the job market.

degree, typically a bachelor's of science, in their selected field. In fact, many jobs in the environmental sciences require a bachelor's degree just to apply. Some available bachelor's specialties include general environmental sciences; environmental studies in botany, statistics, or law; zoology; geology; environmental engineering; and global climate change. But there are many additional specialties available connected to the environmental sciences, such as climatology, forestry, and meteorology. Like associate's degrees, bachelor's degrees are undergraduate degrees.

Bachelor's degrees are usually called four-year degrees, but depending on their program requirements, students may take additional or fewer years to complete one. Earning a bachelor's degree is a good foundation for many career opportunities in the environmental sciences. The field is growing quickly, with 24 percent more environmental science degrees awarded in 2022 than in 2016. Graduates find jobs in diverse fields, ranging from more traditional jobs, such as those in science and forestry, to newer sectors, such as health care, information technology, and marketing. However, one major con of a bachelor's degree is the rising cost of college. The average cost in the United States is $38,270, with some private colleges and universities costing significantly more. However, college saving plans, financial aid, scholarships, grants, student loans, and other resources exist to help with the financial burden.

Master's degree. After earning a bachelor's degree, some people want to continue their education. A master's degree, which is an advanced or graduate degree, is one option to do so. Many professionals, such as soil scientists, environmental economists, water resources specialists, and climate change policy analysts, may seek advanced degrees, especially because many specialized jobs such as these require them. It takes around two years to finish a master's program, though the exact time depends on the program. Master's degrees can cost about as much or sometimes more than a bachelor's program, but many people work while going to school, which helps with the expense. The salaries at jobs that require a master's degree are also often higher than those that require less education. Many colleges employ students in their master's program as undergraduate teacher's aides too. Coursework and fieldwork, a thesis or final paper, an oral examination, and a research project may be required for graduation.

Doctorate. As in a master's program, people seeking a doctorate degree must first earn a bachelor's degree. Then they can apply to a doctorate program to advance their education even further. Doctorate programs are often available in the same specializations as master's programs, such as marine biology, ecology, and more. These graduate programs are rigorous and require a significant time commitment, including both classwork and fieldwork, spanning an average of four to seven years. But they can be a good option for people who want to conduct research or teach the next generation of environmental scientists. For example, a doctorate is usually required to teach at a university.

Doctorate programs are often expensive, though student loans, scholarships, and other financial aid can help cover the cost. And top degree holders are usually directors in their field, netting them higher salaries too. Additionally, many companies jump to hire recent doctorate graduates, even if their area of focus is outside the company's focus, because the writing, research, presentation, and time-management skills needed to earn this degree carry over to any job.

Military. The military offers programs that allow you to serve your country, earn money, and learn a skill all at the same time. GI Bill benefits help service members pay for undergraduate programs, graduate school, and other training during or after their military service is complete. Plus, several military branches seek trained environmental science graduates. For instance, the US Navy seeks environmental health officers to support their efforts in preventing the transmission of viruses and biological agents.

CHAPTER FIVE

The Future

If you've chosen to follow a career path in the environmental sciences, there will likely be many opportunities for you. Changes in Earth's climate, concerns about resource demand and use, and other environmental concerns mean jobs in areas such as climate science and sustainability will continue to be available. Environmental health, which involves identifying and minimizing health impacts from the world around us, is a growing field, especially due to ongoing technological advancements and the continued need for government regulations protecting the environment. Climate change is a real threat that needs experts who can advise policymakers to enact change. And, especially after the start of the COVID-19 pandemic, the importance of public health officials around the globe has been brought to light. Plus, we will likely always need people such as meteorologists to help forecast and understand weather, park rangers to work on federally protected lands, marine biologists to study the ocean, and more.

Careers that provide alternative or renewable energy sources are also expected to increase. Wind turbine service technicians and solar panel installers will be needed as interest and demand for renewable energy sources increase. Those careers are expected to see growth until at least 2029. And if you have installers and technicians, other related professionals are necessary to support them and provide the renewable energy-creating structures. For example, scientists and engineers are needed to write reports on the effectiveness of such structures, work on improvements to them, and develop the next generation of that technology. Workers must manufacture, install, and maintain those energy sources as well.

In 2022 clean energy jobs grew in every state, with nearly three hundred thousand jobs added to the field. Elected in 2020, US President Joe Biden committed to achieving a carbon pollution-free power sector by 2035 and an economy with net-zero emissions by 2050 at the latest. That means that the amount of greenhouse gas produced should be equal—or less—than what is removed from the atmosphere by 2050. The energy sector involves every industry that produces and sells energy, including coal, oil, and gas. By investing in solar, wind, and other clean energy sources, the Earth will be cleaner—and green energy jobs will continue to grow.

All told, according to the US Bureau of Labor Statistics, job growth in occupations related to helping the environment or conserving natural resources is expected to increase by 6 percent between 2022 and 2032. That is faster than average for most careers.

Water quality is an important sector of the environmental sciences.

The Impact of Technology

Technology has made the internet more widely available and put personal electronic devices in the hands of many people. A growing number of machines such as drones and robots have become common and use artificial intelligence (AI). Changes are ongoing in environmental science careers due to such advances in technology.

Robots and drones have many uses. They allow people to see things through artificial eyes when it's not safe for human observation. Simulations are also now possible through the

Opening Up the Environment

Environmental science is one of the least diverse fields of science. Only about 38 percent of environmental scientists are women. And as of 2022, less than 5 percent of environmental professionals identified as Black, Asian, or another marginalized race or ethnicity, even though those groups make up nearly 40 percent of the total US population and are more likely to live in places affected by environmental issues including pollution, limited access to clean water, and more. "I go to conferences and I'm often the only person of color in the room," Esther Ngumbi, a professor of food security and entomology, said. "You sit in a classroom and all the scientists that are being introduced are white, white, white. And then you sit there as a Black student, and you ask, 'Do I even have a place in science?'"

One World Science, a scientific outreach initiative, cites high costs of further education, unpaid internships being difficult or even impossible for lower-income students to accept, and recruitment efforts often not reaching people of color or low-income students as reasons for this lack of diversity. Many universities are committing to expanding diversity, equity, and inclusion in the sciences. And organizations are working to address the lack of diversity and opportunities in the environmental sciences too. Environmental Science Without Borders connects professionals in the industry with students and scientists in developing countries. The National Oceanic and Atmospheric Administration has also put forth a strategy to implement programs and policies encouraging underrepresented groups to enter the field. Organizations such as these are helping ensure that more people will be represented in the environmental sciences in the future.

use of virtual reality (VR), such as by creating a virtual model of an ecosystem. Many of these same technologies are used for entertainment. You may have played with a drone or robot or used virtual reality in a game, a museum, a theater, an amusement park, or a concert. In new professional applications, scientists and other workers are bringing these advances to life to help study and protect the environment.

An example of the positive role of AI in the environmental sciences is its use to understand how solar energy facilities impact birds. The research and development center Oak Ridge National Laboratory found that "solar energy development could impact birds, but field surveys of bird carcasses [at solar panel farms] do not provide sufficient data to accurately understand the nature and magnitude of impact. Because data collection does not take place in real time, these methods cannot observe bird behavior around solar panels that could indicate causes of fatality, sources of attraction, and potential benefits to birds." AI in cameras can help figure out what's actually happening. The cameras monitor birds from sunrise to sunset, detecting and tracking different species of birds using four AI models. It records collisions and notifies people about them. With this tool, humans can spend more time verifying ongoing incidents, rather than waiting for them to occur.

Robots clean litter from the floor of the ocean. According to the SeaClear Project, which focused on cleaning trash from the oceans, "today's oceans contain 26–66 million tons (23.6 to 60 million metric tons) of waste, with approximately 94 percent located on the seafloor. So far, collection efforts have focused mostly on surface waste. The few efforts to gather underwater waste involve human divers who are put

Green Growth

Committing to net-zero emissions means that fields that manufacture clean energy technology will grow significantly, with as many as 5.7 million new jobs created by 2035. Here is how much each energy sector could potentially grow between 2020 and 2035:

Summary of Employment Impacts		
Energy Sector	**Jobs in 2020**	**Jobs by 2035**
Electricity—solar	100,670	2,548,918
Building—electricity, residential	264,603	1,103,502
Transportation—alternative vehicles	309,912	3,651,432
Fuel—hydrogen	29	369,025

Some people fear that a rise in net-zero emissions will lead to loss of jobs in other sectors, such as fossil fuels or coal manufacturing. Growth in the green version of those sectors—such as hydrogen energy—does not yet match those losses. However, the skills, education, and experience needed to work in any of those careers are transferrable between industries and jobs. And as scientists continue to develop new energy technology, job opportunities may continue to change too.

in potential danger." When robots clear ocean floors, they protect the human professionals who might have done the job instead.

Drones can be used for many purposes for studying our surroundings. Then researchers and scientists can study the environmental data they collect. For example, they can survey large areas quickly and reach areas that a human may have trouble reaching. Oak Ridge National Laboratory used drones to identify mercury in streams. Mercury is a dangerous pollutant. According to the laboratory, "drones can use cameras and other sensors to collect information about the Earth, finding things a researcher on foot may not be able to see."

Virtual reality also has many applications that apply to the environmental sciences. One example is the Centers for Disease Control and Prevention's use of VR to train staff to set up a biologically safe cabinet for use in a contaminated area during a crisis. The simulated environment allowed them to practice without exposure to real contaminants.

These are just a few of the technologies that put more tools in the toolbox for environmental scientists. Who knows what the future may hold for your career in the environmental sciences?

CONCLUSION

A Spot for Everyone

Throughout this book, you've been introduced to environmental science jobs you may have never heard of or learned more about careers you've been interested in for most of your life. You may see yourself building, maintaining, monitoring, investigating, advising, teaching, or protecting and preserving our natural resources. There are career paths right out of high school and career paths that require higher education. There are career paths that have you working with people, with animals, with both, or with neither.

No matter what environmental science discipline sounds most exciting to you, it's time to do further research. You might conduct an informational interview with someone, visit a college campus with a program in your area of interest, or do something else. Here are a few reminders of next steps that might help you on your career journey:

- Use the many online and public resources available to you to get started.

Environmental scientists ensure the future is clean, safe, and sustainable.

- Reach out to trusted adults and organizations for more support and information.
- Use social media and informational sites to expand your understanding of a career.
- Journal or otherwise record your career investigation.
- When you feel a pull toward a career, try to learn more about it.

Planning for a career can feel daunting. But it can also be fun, exciting, and rewarding! Remember that it's worth putting in the time to find a career that fits your goals.

GLOSSARY

air quality: the degree of air cleanliness for humans and the environment

animal husbandry: the management, care, and breeding of animals

animal welfare: the well-being of non-human animals

artificial intelligence (AI): machines and computers that perform functions that normally require human intelligence

biodegradable: an organic object that can be broken down by bacteria or other living organisms

biodiversity: the variety of life on Earth, especially within a habitat or ecosystem

biomass: the amount of living matter in an area

botany: the branch of biology dealing with plants

climate change: significant and long-lasting change in Earth's climate and weather patterns, often associated with global warming

elective: an optional class or course that a student chooses

endangered species: a species threatened with extinction

entomology: a branch of science that studies insects

forensic: the scientific analysis of physical evidence

game preserve: an area of land where hunting and fishing are carefully controlled

geology: the branch of science that studies Earth's structure and makeup, its history, and how it changes over time

GI Bill: a law that provides benefits for qualified veterans to help them pay for school or training

graduate: a program of a student at a college or university who is engaging in studies beyond their first or bachelor's degree

greenhouse gas: a gas that absorbs infrared radiation, such as carbon dioxide or chlorofluorocarbons, and raises the surface temperature of the planet

habitat: the place or environment where people, animals, or plants typically live and grow

hydrogen energy: a form of clean energy. Hydrogen is the most abundant chemical element in nature, and, when used in a fuel cell, its only by-product is water.

infrastructure: the structures and systems that serve a country, city, or other area, such as roads, power lines, bridges, schools, and hospitals

marginalized: a person, group, or idea treated as insignificant or powerless

median: the value of the number in a set where half of the remaining numbers are above and half are below

net-zero emissions: a goal where the rate of human-produced greenhouse gas emissions is in balance with how fast they are removed from the environment

nonprofit: an organization that operates to benefit the public, rather than as a business with the goal to earn profits for the owners

sector: a group of companies or industries that share similarities in goals, activities, products, or services

species: a class of beings sharing common attributes and name, such as the human race

statistics: a branch of mathematics that collects, analyzes, and summarizes numerical data

steward: one who manages or oversees the well-being of something

sustainable: capable of being maintained at length without interruption or weakening

thesis: a long essay on a particular subject that involves personal research. Theses are usually written by candidates for an academic degree or a professional certification.

undergraduate: a program of a student at a college or university who has not received their first degree, especially a bachelor's degree

urban sprawl: the spread of towns and cities onto previously undeveloped land

weatherization: making something better protected against weather

wind turbine: a wind-driven engine that generates electricity

SOURCE NOTES

8 "We save nature . . . nature saves us.": Paul Salopek, "Green Hindus," *National Geographic, Out of Eden Walk*, August 6, 2018, https://outofedenwalk.nationalgeographic.org/articles/2018-08-green-hindus.

27 "All infrastructure, everything . . . come to love.": Shannon Rooney, "Considering Civil Engineering? Three Students on Why They Chose the Major and What They Love About It," University of Notre Dame, August 23, 2023, https://admissions.nd.edu/visit-engage/stories-news/considering-civil-engineering-students-on-why-they-chose-the-major-and-what-they-love-about-it/.

28 "Noticed a pattern . . . capabilities, or potential.": CareerExplorer by sokanu, accessed June 30, 2024, https://www.careerexplorer.com/about/.

40 "Seventy-two percent reported . . . could be pursued.": Scott Jaschik, "Are High School Grads Prepared?" *Inside Higher Ed*, December 4, 2022, https://www.insidehighered.com/admissions/article/2022/12/05/survey-shows-many-high-school-graduates-are-uncertain.

50 "I go to . . . place in science?": Hiroko Tabuchi and Tatiana Schlossberg, "As Scientists, We Have Yet to Close the Racial Disparities," *New York Times*, June 10, 2020, https://www.nytimes.com/2020/06/10/climate/climate-scientists-strike-black-lives-matter.html.

51 "Solar energy development . . . benefits to birds.": "AI-Enabled Avian-Solar Interaction Monitoring," Argonne National Laboratory, accessed June 30, 2024, https://www.anl.gov/evs/avian-solar.

53 "Today's oceans contain . . . in potential danger.": "SeaClear," accessed June 30, 2024, https://seaclear-project.eu/.

53 "Drones can use . . . able to see.": "Drones Give Bird's Eye View for Collecting Environmental and Security Data," Oak Ridge National Laboratory, March 14, 2023, https://www.ornl.gov/news/drones-give-birds-eye-view-collecting-environmental-and-security-data.

SELECTED BIBLIOGRAPHY

"About NRCS." Natural Resources Conservation Service. Accessed April 11, 2024. https://www.nrcs.usda.gov/about.

Gemeš, Nikola. "Top 21 Climate Change Jobs That Will Save the World." GreenCitizen, February 22, 2021. https://greencitizen.com/blog/climate-change-jobs/#20_Climatologist.

Hubbart, Sarah. "Explore Career Opportunities in Environmental Science." National Environmental Education Foundation, April 28, 2021. https://www.neefusa.org/story/environmental-education/explore-career-opportunities-environmental-science.

"A Timeline of Environmental History." Encyclopedia Britannica. Accessed April 11, 2024. https://www.britannica.com/story/a-timeline-of-environmental-history.

"Top 8 Reasons to Pursue an Environmental Engineering Degree." Central Michigan University. Accessed April 11, 2024. https://www.cmich.edu/blog/all-things-higher-ed/reasons-to-pursue-environmental-engineering-degree.

"United Nations Sustainable Development." United Nations. Accessed April 11, 2024. https://www.un.org/sustainabledevelopment/.

FURTHER INFORMATION

Books

Hicks, Seth. *Career Planning for Teens: Discover the Proven Path to Finding a Successful Career That's Right for You.* Monee, IL: Canyon Press, 2022.
This book helps teens as they're planning a career. It helps them consider their interests, narrow options, choose a career path, and develop a road map.

Ingram, Alexa. *Climate Change Simplified.* Coppell, TX: Authentic EcoPress, 2023.
This book focuses on global warming and people's carbon footprints. It shares specific tips that can affect a person's impact on global warming.

Saidian, Siyavush. *Careers for People Who Love the Great Outdoors.* New York: Rosen, 2021.
This book covers many environmental careers. If you can't imagine working in an office, this book introduces some outdoor careers that might interest you.

Small, Cathleen. *How to Choose Your Perfect Engineering Career.* Bridgnorth, Shropshire, UK: Cheriton Children's Books, 2023.
This book helps students explore their interests, personality type, likes and dislikes, and hopes for the future so they can navigate a pathway to their ideal engineering career. It includes flowchart quizzes that allow the reader to narrow down their options and find a route that is right for them.

Taberham, Justin. *Global Environmental Careers: The Worldwide Green Jobs Resource.* Hoboken, NJ: John Wiley & Sons Ltd, 2022.
This book is filled with practical advice and current information on the global environmental sector.

Websites

AI-Enabled Avian-Solar Interaction Monitoring

https://www.anl.gov/evs/avian-solar

This United States Department of Energy site contains an explanation of how AI is used to study the impact of solar energy facilities on birds.

Career Opportunities in Environmental Science

https://www.neefusa.org/story/environmental-education/explore-career-opportunities-environmental-science

This website provides resources for exploring career opportunities in environmental science. The site is the home of the National Environmental Education Foundation, which supports learning and exploration for people to learn about the environment.

Climate Change Jobs that Will Save the World

https://greencitizen.com/

Green Citizen offers information about environmental issues and sustainability. It hosts articles, resources, and more about green living.

Natural Resources Conservation

https://www.nrcs.usda.gov/conservation-basics/natural-resource-concerns

The US Department of Agriculture runs the website for the Natural Resources Conservation, which features information about the basics of conservation and different conservation focus areas. You can also find specific information about your state.

Park Ranger

https://careers.doi.gov/occupational-series/park-ranger

Featuring great information about the pathway to work as a park ranger, this Department of the Interior website explains what park rangers are, what education is required to become one, what skills park rangers need, and more.

INDEX

agriculture, 6–7, 26, 43
air quality, 23–25, 32
animal biology, 6
animal welfare, 18, 20
apprenticeships, 42
apps, 35
artificial intelligence (AI), 49, 51
associate degree, 23, 43–44
atmospheric scientist, 15

biodiversity, 20
biomass, 23
Bishnoi people, 8

Carver, George Washington, 12
Catlin, George, 19
certifications, 24
citizen science, 35
clean energy, 22, 48, 52
Clean Water Act, 10
climate change, 17, 20, 44–45, 47
climate emergencies, 16
climate science, 47
climatologist, 16
colleges, 41, 43, 45
conservationists, 19, 21
Conservation Job Board, 30
conserving energy, 16

disaster preparedness, 16
disaster relief, 26, 38
drones, 49, 51, 53

Earth Day, 9
ecologists, 19
economics, 48
ecosystems, 6, 8, 13, 27, 35
electricians, 14
electricity, 13, 52
endangered species, 9, 11, 18
energy auditing, 16
engineers, 10–11, 24, 26–27, 37, 41, 48
environmental engineering, 4, 11, 20, 24, 44
environmental health, 11, 23, 46
environmentalists, 8
Environmental Protection Agency (EPA), 9–10, 16, 24, 42
Environmental Response, Compensation, and Liability Act, 10

fieldwork, 45, 46
forensics, 21
forestry, 6, 44–45

game wardens, 20, 38
green careers, 14, 26
green economies, 20
guidance counselors, 41

habitats, 18, 20, 21

internships, 42–43, 50
interviews, 8, 32–33, 54

job growth, 48

law enforcement, 20
litter, 13, 51

marketing, 45
master's degree, 17, 23, 45
meteorology, 4, 44
military, 46

National Oceanic and Atmospheric Administration, 35, 50
national parks, 13, 19, 21
natural resources, 12, 14, 20, 22, 48, 54
nonprofits, 13, 23, 34–35

Oak Ridge National Laboratory, 51, 53

park rangers, 21, 31, 47
pay, 4, 25–26, 42, 46
policymakers, 47
pollution, 8–9, 16, 20, 22–24, 27, 36, 48, 50
preservation, 14
public health, 6, 25, 47

recycling, 13, 21, 34
research, 9, 12–13, 16–17, 19, 25, 27, 31, 34–35, 38–39, 45–46, 51, 54
resource management, 20
robots, 49, 51, 53
rules and regulations, 24, 47

salaries, 15–17, 20–21, 23–25, 27, 30, 38, 45–46
Silent Spring, 8
soil conservation, 12
solar panels, 14, 16, 23, 39, 48, 51
sustainability, 11, 21–22, 47

technicians, 14, 21, 42, 48
toxic waste, 10–11

undergraduate degree, 23
United Nations Environment Programme (UNEP), 20
United States Department of the Interior, 21
United States Geological Survey, 16
urban green spaces, 22

volunteering, 13, 34–35

water quality, 10
weather, 4, 13–16, 35, 47
weatherization expert, 16
wildlife, 11, 14, 17–18, 20–21, 38
wind turbines, 14, 23, 48
World Environment Day, 20
World Wildlife Fund, 13

ABOUT THE AUTHOR

Sherry Howard is a freelance author from Middletown, Kentucky. She enjoys writing poetry, fiction, and nonfiction for children. When she's not writing, you might find her chatting with grandchildren, playing with pampered pups, enjoying the fish's colors in her aquariums, or feeding a bearded dragon named Kuda. She's a big fan of southern front porches, the roar of ocean waves, and the wisdom of Yoda.

PHOTO ACKNOWLEDGMENTS

Image credits: simonkr/E+/Getty Images, p.5; PATRICK HERTZOG/AFP/Getty Images, p.7; Keith Edward Byron/Fairfax Media Archives/Getty Images, p.9; Jevtic/iStock/Getty Images, p.10; Hulton Archive/Archive Photos/Getty Images, p.12; Antonio Busiello/Moment/Getty Images, p.13; supersizer/E+/Getty Images, p.15; Unya-MT/iStock/Getty Images, p.17; LUCIE AUBOURG/AFP/Getty Imaes, p.18; MARTIN SYLVEST/Ritzau Scanpix/AFP/Getty Images, p.20; Nansan Houn/iStock/Getty Images, p.21; Tony Skert/Shutterstock, p.25; nd3000/iStock/Getty Images, p.29; Cast of Thousands/Shutterstock, p.30; Yellow Dog Productions/Photodisc/, p.32; SDI Productions/E+/Getty Images, p.37; Cast of Thousands/Shutterstock, p.39; Thurtell/E+/Getty Images, p.41; hxyume/E+/Getty Images, p.44; PixeloneStocker/Moment/Getty Images, p.49; ZU_09/E+/Getty Images, p.52; DSCimage/iStock/Getty Images, p.55.

Cover image: owngarden/Getty Images